The United Methodist Church

Developed by the
Christian Education Staff
of The General Board of Discipleship
of The United Methodist Church

DISCIPLESHIP RESOURCES

P.O. BOX 340003 • NASHVILLE, TN 37203-0003
www.discipleshipresources.org

This booklet was developed by the Christian Education Staff of The General Board of Discipleship of The United Methodist Church. It is one in a series of booklets designed to provide essential knowledge for teachers. Members of the staff who helped write and develop this series are Terry Carty, Bill Crenshaw, Donna Gaither, Rick Gentzler, Mary Alice Gran, Susan Hay, Betsey Heavner, Diana Hynson, Carol Krau, MaryJane Pierce Norton, Deb Smith, Julia Wallace, and Linda Whited.

Cover and booklet design by Joey McNair
Cover illustration by Mike Drake
Edited by Debra D. Smith and Heidi L. Hewitt

ISBN 0-88177-363-8

DR363

Contents

This booklet is dedicated to
YOU,
a teacher of
children, youth, or adults,
WHO,
with fear, excitement, joy,
and commitment,
allows God to lead you
in the call to
TEACH.

The gifts he gave were that some would be . . .
teachers . . . for building up the body of Christ.
(Ephesians 4:11-12)

Introduction

In accepting the invitation to teach in your congregation, you have entered into a time of growing as a Christian while you lead others to grow along with you. Whether you are a teacher of children, youth, or adults, it is important that you know something about the church where you are and how your class members learn and worship.

This booklet introduces basic knowledge about the history, mission, and structure of The United Methodist Church and information about the words and symbols that you see in your church and on the resources your church develops. Depending on your background, this booklet may be a crash course on United Methodist basics, a reminder of things you have forgotten, or an encouragement to continue to learn more about your church.

Teachers and small-group leaders are growing in faith. As teachers, we pay attention to our relationships with God and with others. We seek to live our faith in our daily lives. We create safe, healthy settings for people to seek God, to respond to God's grace, and to find support and encouragement for living as disciples in the world.

Growing in faith, which helps us become spiritual leaders, is a life-changing experience that continues throughout life. We do not have this experience alone. We grow with the help of God and with the help of our congregation as they support us by providing opportunities for learning, resources for teaching, prayer, and training.

This booklet about The United Methodist Church is one of ten booklets that will equip you for teaching. Use the entire series to reinforce your own knowledge, skills, and abilities.

Other booklets in this series are
What Every Teacher Needs to Know About
- *the Bible*
- *Christian Heritage*
- *Classroom Environment*
- *Curriculum*
- *Faith Language*
- *Living the Faith*
- *People*
- *Teaching*
- *Theology*

History

Go...make disciples of all nations.

(Matthew 28:19)

The mission of The United Methodist Church is "to make disciples of Jesus Christ" (*The Book of Discipline of The United Methodist Church—2000,* ¶ 120). The mission had its beginnings in the eighteenth-century movement that in 1968 became The United Methodist Church. John Wesley was the founder of that movement.

John Wesley

John Wesley was born in 1703 in Epworth, England. He was one of many children of Samuel Wesley, an Anglican priest, and Susanna Wesley, a strong, caring, Christian woman. John Wesley studied at Christ Church College in Oxford, England. In 1728, at the age of twenty-five, John Wesley was ordained as a priest in the Church of England.

The Holy Club

While John and his brother Charles Wesley were at Oxford, they organized and led a group of Oxford students who became known as the Holy Club. The members of the club met regularly for Bible study, prayer, social work, fasting, and Holy Communion. They practiced their faith by visiting people in prison, by taking care of people who were poor, and by showing concern for the social issues of their day.

John and Charles in America

In 1735, John and Charles left for America with dreams of becoming missionaries. But their efforts failed, and they returned to England in about two years. They both returned searching for something more in their own faith.

A Heart-Warming Experience

May 24, 1738, marked a turning point in John's faith. After attending a religious service on Aldersgate-Street in London, John wrote in his journal:

In the evening, I went very unwillingly to a society in Aldersgate-Street, where one was reading Luther's preface to the Epistle to the Romans. About a quarter before nine, while he was describing the change which God works in the heart through faith in Christ, I felt my heart strangely warmed. I felt I did trust in Christ, Christ alone, for salvation: And an assurance was given me, that he had taken away my sins, even mine, and saved me from the law of sin and death.

John Wesley's heart-warming experience came only three days after his brother Charles had found God's peace in a similar experience.

Preaching in Streets and Fields

Soon, John and Charles and George Whitefield, their friend from the Holy Club, began preaching to the poor in England. Since their preaching was not encouraged inside the Church of England, they preached in the streets, in abandoned buildings, in homes, in mines, and in open fields.

Early Methodist Societies

John Wesley organized the converts into societies. These groups were based on Wesley's experience with the Holy Club at Oxford, on his observations of the Moravians who had influenced his faith, and on other Anglican religious societies. The societies met weekly for preaching, prayer, hymn-singing, Bible study, Christian conversation, and mutual accountability for their spiritual growth.

Anyone who wanted to "flee from the wrath to come, and to be saved from their sins" was welcome to join a Methodist society and lead a disciplined Christian life. Each person was required to follow three General Rules, which are still expected of United Methodists today:

- Do no harm.
- Do good.
- Attend the ordinances of God.

The ordinances of God are those things that help us experience God's presence. They include worship, prayer, Scripture study, Holy Communion, and fasting.

Later, the societies were broken up into even smaller groups called classes and bands. In these smaller groups, members talked about their lives, confessed their sins, prayed for one another, and encouraged one another to be more-faithful Christians.

John Wesley never intended for the societies to become a new church. He himself remained a priest in the Church of England until his death. The members of the societies, classes, and bands were encouraged to attend the services of the local Church of England and to receive Holy Communion there. However, as the Methodist societies grew, they took on more and more of the feel of a separate church. Although Wesley had originally intended that the Methodists should remain members of the Church of England, a new church seemed inevitable.

Methodist Societies in America

Methodist societies developed in America as a lay movement.

- Robert Strawbridge started what Francis Asbury described as "the first society in Maryland—and America."
- Barbara Heck and Philip Embury began a society in New York at about the same time.
- Thomas Webb introduced Methodism on Long Island, in Philadelphia, and in other places.

John Wesley sent missionaries to America in 1769. During the Revolutionary War, though, John Wesley supported England. As a result, all of the British Methodist preachers—except Francis Asbury—returned to England. Asbury continued to preach in America, riding thousands of miles each year to organize new churches. By 1784, the Methodist movement in America had grown to 15,000 members.

The First American Conference

In 1784, John Wesley began ordaining lay preachers to spread the work of the Methodist movement in the United States. It was not an easy decision for Wesley to make. He knew that by ordaining ministers for the United States church, he would be sanctioning a new church that would no longer be part of the Church of England.

In that same year, a conference of Methodist preachers was held at Lovely Lane Chapel in Baltimore, Maryland, on Christmas Eve. At this conference

- the name Methodist Episcopal Church in America was adopted (Episcopal means that the church structure includes bishops as leaders.);
- Francis Asbury was elected as superintendent and joined Thomas Coke, the superintendent sent from England by John Wesley (Superintendents were later called bishops.);
- the first *Book of Discipline* was adopted.

The *Discipline* stated that the new church would bring John Wesley's goals for England to America: "to reform the continent and to spread scriptural holiness through these lands."

Circuit Riders

In the years that followed, the Methodist preachers were circuit riders, traveling miles upon miles to take the gospel of Jesus Christ into every part of the United States. These circuits were modeled after the system that John Wesley had devised for the English societies. Francis Asbury brought the circuit system to the United States, where it was especially well suited to the American frontier. The Methodist plan for circuit riders helped establish the new Methodist Episcopal Church firmly in American soil.

United Brethren in Christ Church

Before John Wesley had sent missionaries to America, the United Brethren in Christ Church had its beginnings in America. In 1752, Philip William Otterbein, who had been born in 1726 in the German town of Dillenburg, set sail for America with five other young German Reformed ministers. Otterbein had spent three years in Ockersdorf, where he had gained a reputation for vigorous, direct preaching, especially stressing regeneration (experiencing a new life in Christ).

Several years later, in 1758, Martin Boehm was chosen by lot to be a minister in his American Mennonite congregation. In 1761, he was advanced to the office of bishop. The Boehm revival began as a result of Boehm's great preaching and testimony.

The meeting of Otterbein and Boehm in 1767 proved to be a decisive factor in the formation of the United Brethren in Christ Church. Otterbein attended a meeting at the farm of Isaac Long in Lancaster County, Pennsylvania. Martin Boehm's preaching reminded Otterbein of his own spiritual experiences and struggles. After Boehm's sermon, Otterbein went forward, embraced Boehm, and exclaimed, "Wir sind Brüder!" (We are brethren!).

Otterbein and Boehm became the first bishops of the United Brethren in Christ Church, which was formed in 1800 and was the first denomination originating in the United States.

Philip William Otterbein and Francis Asbury worked in close fellowship. In fact, Otterbein, at Asbury's request, participated in the laying on of hands at Asbury's ordination. However, there were two significant reasons that these men did not join their organizations in the early 1800's: (1) a difference in the concept of authority and (2) a difference in language. Asbury was aggressive in establishing orderly rules and regarded them as having weighty authority. Otterbein was also a man of order; however, he did not impose his authority in a weighty manner, either as pastor of his congregation or later as bishop of The United Brethren Church. And as related to language, Asbury and the Methodists spoke English, while Otterbein and the United Brethren spoke German.

The Evangelical Church

Jacob Albright, the founder of what later became The Evangelical Church, began his ministry by studying the Bible in German. When several of his children died in an epidemic of dysentery in 1790, Albright experienced a crisis in his faith. But in the summer of 1791, he received a conversion experience at a prayer meeting where he is quoted as saying, "All fear and anxiety of heart disappeared. Joy and blessed peace inbreathed my breast. God gave witness to my spirit that I had become a child of God."

Although Albright was Lutheran, he joined a Methodist class because he enjoyed the Methodists' orderly approach to religion. However, since Albright spoke little English, he found it difficult to worship with the Methodists.

At the urging of his friends, Albright became an itinerant preacher. During his first four years, Albright gained converts in many places, cautioning people of faith to seek salvation through a genuine change of heart rather than through their churches' traditions, forms, and ceremonies.

In 1800, Albright gathered a number of converts and formed three classes after the manner of the Methodist classes. From this early beginning would later be formed The Evangelical Association. Following a division and then a reunion in 1922, the body later became The Evangelical Church.

Evangelical United Brethren

Otterbein's and Boehm's United Brethren in Christ Church and Albright's Evangelical Church decided to unite as one body in 1946. The two groups joined to form The Evangelical United Brethren Church, known as the EUB Church. The EUB churches were primarily in the Mid-Atlantic and Midwest states (Pennsylvania, Maryland, Ohio, Indiana, Nebraska, and so forth).

The Methodist Episcopal Church

Meanwhile, during the years that led to the formation of The Evangelical United Brethren Church, The Methodist Episcopal Church had its own problems and divisions over such issues as church authority and slavery.

- Methodist Protestant Church—split over the question of the role and authority of lay people in the church.
- Methodist Episcopal Church, South—split over the issue of slavery.

The Methodist Church

The Methodist Church was formed in 1939 when The Methodist Episcopal Church, The Methodist Episcopal Church, South, and The Methodist Protestant Church became one in a historic Uniting Conference.

African-American Methodists

The Methodist Church from its beginnings included African Americans. The first Methodist societies—the one in New York established by Philip Embury and Barbara Heck and the one established by Robert Strawbridge in Maryland—had members who were African-American slaves. After 1786, when membership reports distinguished between white and black members, the numbers were often almost equal.

Although the 1800 *Discipline* did not record the action, ordination of African-American deacons was approved at the 1800 General Conference. The ordination of African-American elders was later approved in 1812.

Perhaps the best known of the African-American preachers of the day was Harry Hosier. Thomas Coke once described Hosier as "one of the best preachers in the world."

Discrimination during the years of slavery and beyond, though, led some African-American Methodists to form new Methodist churches of their own.

- The African Methodist Episcopal Church (AME) was founded by Richard Allen and Daniel Coker in 1816.
- The African Methodist Episcopal Zion Church (AME Zion), started in New York, became official in 1822 when white elders who had withdrawn from The Methodist Episcopal Church ordained elders for the Zion Church.

- The Colored Methodist Episcopal Church (CME) was established in 1870 by the General Conference of The Methodist Episcopal Church, South. The organizing delegates dropped the word *South* from the name that was originally intended for the church. Then, in 1954, the name was changed to The Christian Methodist Episcopal Church.

The United Methodist Church

On April 23, 1968, in Dallas, Texas, The Evangelical United Brethren Church and The Methodist Church united to create a new denomination: The United Methodist Church. On that day, these two churches with similar backgrounds and theology—who had historically been separated largely by language differences—became one.

Today, United Methodist congregations are found not only in the United States but in many countries throughout the world.

The United Methodist Church is a church that celebrates its diversity. Our church is in rural and urban areas, and the members include people from all ethnic groups. Though our congregations vary in size, location, and cultural background, they share a common heritage as United Methodists.

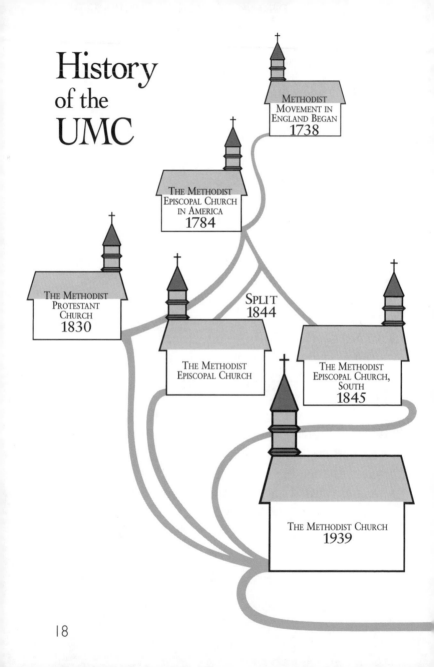

History
of the
UMC

METHODIST MOVEMENT IN ENGLAND BEGAN
1738

THE METHODIST EPISCOPAL CHURCH IN AMERICA
1784

THE METHODIST PROTESTANT CHURCH
1830

SPLIT
1844

THE METHODIST EPISCOPAL CHURCH

THE METHODIST EPISCOPAL CHURCH, SOUTH
1845

THE METHODIST CHURCH
1939

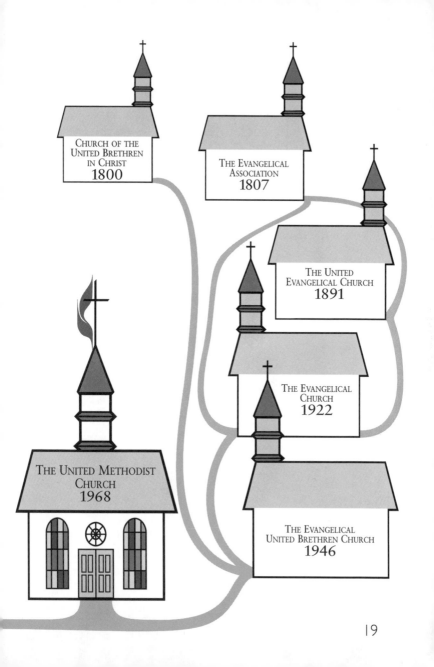

CHURCH OF THE
UNITED BRETHREN
IN CHRIST
1800

THE EVANGELICAL
ASSOCIATION
1807

THE UNITED
EVANGELICAL CHURCH
1891

THE EVANGELICAL
CHURCH
1922

THE EVANGELICAL
UNITED BRETHREN CHURCH
1946

THE UNITED METHODIST
CHURCH
1968

For Personal Reflection

What do you know about the history of your own congregation? When was it begun? Was it originally a Methodist Church or an Evangelical United Brethren Church? Ask someone who has been a member of your congregation for many years to tell you about important events in the life of the congregation. Use the space below for your reflections.

Mission

The mission of the Church is to make disciples of Jesus Christ.

(*Book of Discipline, 2000*; ¶ 120)

Although making disciples was clearly defined as the mission of The United Methodist Church at the General Conference of 1996, making disciples has been the mission of the church since Jesus' Great Commission (Matthew 28:19). Making disciples is a mission that reaches back to the beginnings of the church's history and also continues to be the focus of the church's ministry today. But what does it mean to make disciples of Jesus Christ? And how does The United Methodist Church approach that task?

The Primary Task

The primary task of the local church is one task (making disciples of Jesus Christ) in four actions: receiving and welcoming people, relating them to God, nurturing them in discipleship, and sending them into ministry in the world.

Our Primary Task

Reach Out & Receive

Relate People to God

Making Disciples

Send Forth to Live Transformed/ Transforming Lives

Nurture & Strengthen in the Christian Faith

Then when disciples are in ministry in the world, the cycle begins again as they receive and welcome even more people.

Methodists in Mission

The United Methodist faith is deeply rooted in the Scripture and in the basic beliefs of all Christians. Out of that theology and the faith have grown some specific actions that mark United Methodists as Christians engaged in ministry to the world. The early members of the groups that eventually became The United Methodist Church

- took strong stands on issues such as slavery, smuggling, and humane treatment of prisoners;
- established institutions for higher learning;
- started hospitals and shelters for children and the elderly;
- founded Goodwill Industries in 1902;
- became actively involved in efforts for world peace;
- adopted a Social Creed and Social Principles to guide them as they relate to God's world and God's people;
- participated with other religious groups in ecumenical efforts to be in mission.

Our Social Creed

We believe in God, Creator of the world; and in Jesus Christ, the Redeemer of creation. We believe in the Holy Spirit, through whom we acknowledge God's gifts, and we repent of our sin in misusing these gifts to idolatrous ends.

We affirm the natural world as God's handiwork and dedicate ourselves to its preservation, enhancement, and faithful use by humankind.

We joyfully receive for ourselves and others the blessings of community, sexuality, marriage, and the family.

We commit ourselves to the rights of men, women, children, youth, young adults, the aging, and people with disabilities; to improvement of the quality of life; and to the rights and dignity of racial, ethnic, and religious minorities.

We believe in the right and duty of persons to work for the glory of God and the good of themselves and others and in the protection of their welfare in so doing; in the rights to property as a trust from God, collective bargaining, and responsible consumption; and in the elimination of economic and social distress.

We dedicate ourselves to peace throughout the world, to the rule of justice and law among nations, and to individual freedom for all people of the world.

We believe in the present and final triumph of God's Word in human affairs and gladly accept our commission to manifest the life of the gospel in the world. Amen.

(From *The Book of Discipline of The United Methodist Church—2000*, ¶ 166.)

The Social Principles

In addition to Our Social Creed, United Methodists seek to create a world of justice. The Social Principles (described in *The Book of Discipline of The United Methodist Church—2000*, ¶¶ 160–65) are divided into six parts that explain how United Methodist Christians are called to live in God's world: Natural World, Nurturing Community, Social Community, Economic Community, Political Community, World Community.

The Book of Resolutions

In addition to the standards in "Our Social Creed" and in the Social Principles, *The Book of Resolutions* is published every four years. This book is a collection of the official policy statements adopted by the General Conference of The United Methodist Church. The statements are guides for the work and ministry of the church, including developing educational resources, relating faith to daily living, and making public the church's official stand on current social issues.

The statements in *The Book of Resolutions* are not legally binding on individual United Methodists, who may take a wide variety of stands on the issues. However, these official statements of the denomination are a resource for reference and study as church members seek to make faithful disciples related to the topics addressed by these official resolutions.

For Personal Reflection

Reflect on the ways your congregation welcomes and receives people, relates them to God, nurtures them in discipleship, and sends them out into ministry in the world. As a teacher, what do you do that contributes to this primary task of the church?

Connectional Structure

Connectionalism…provides…opportunities to carry out our mission in unity and strength.

(*Book of Discipline, 2000;* ¶ 701)

The United Methodist Church is uniquely structured to carry out its mission of making disciples. All local churches, the centers where the mission of making disciples is most likely to be fulfilled, are linked through an organization called the connectional system.

What Does Connectional Mean?

Connectional simply means that all United Methodist churches are linked to all other United Methodist churches by organization and by purpose as they go about the work of making disciples.

John Wesley listed Christian conferencing among the spiritual disciplines through which God's grace may be made known to us. Within the structure of The United Methodist Church are groupings of people or churches called conferences: charge conferences, annual conferences, jurisdictional conferences, central conferences,

General Conference. At these conference meetings, United Methodists gather to discuss important issues for the church; that is, they join together in Christian conferencing to listen for God's call and to discover God's will for the church. When you hear and see the word *conference*, remember that it refers to both the actual assembly of people and to the process of seeking God's grace together.

Note this diagram of the structure of The United Methodist Church—a structure that encourages Christian conferencing at every level.

Organizational Connections

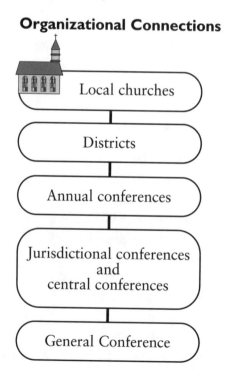

Local churches

Districts

Annual conferences

Jurisdictional conferences
and
central conferences

General Conference

Leadership Connections

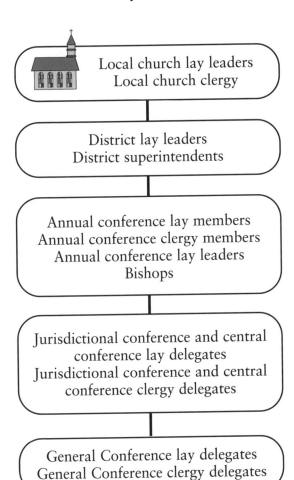

Local church lay leaders
Local church clergy

District lay leaders
District superintendents

Annual conference lay members
Annual conference clergy members
Annual conference lay leaders
Bishops

Jurisdictional conference and central
conference lay delegates
Jurisdictional conference and central
conference clergy delegates

General Conference lay delegates
General Conference clergy delegates

The Local Church

Ministry begins at the local church level. Each congregation has an elected lay leader, who works with other lay and clergy leaders to carry out the mission of the church.

Districts

Groups of churches in a geographic area are organized to form a district, somewhat similar to the way cities and towns are organized into counties. Often, churches in a district will work together to provide training and mission opportunities. Each district has a district lay leader, who supports and trains local church lay leaders. A district superintendent is a clergy person who is appointed to provide administrative and spiritual leadership for the churches in a district.

Annual Conference

All the districts in a particular geographic area make up an annual conference. The words *annual conference* can refer either to the geographic area that makes up the conference or to the annual meeting of lay and clergy members of the annual conference.

Each local charge elects at least one lay member of the annual conference. The annual conference includes equal numbers of clergy and lay people. So, if a congregation is served by two clergy, then the congregation would also have two lay members of the annual conference.

A bishop presides over an annual conference. The bishop, in consultation with district superintendents and local churches, appoints the clergy who will serve the local congregations within that annual conference.

Annual conferences support the work of the local church and help local churches be in ministry in the larger community. Many annual conferences operate camps and sponsor other mission opportunities for churches in the conference.

Jurisdictional Conference

Annual conferences in the United States are divided into five jurisdictions: Northeastern, Southeastern, North Central, South Central, and Western. Each jurisdiction has a jurisdictional conference every four years. Equal numbers of lay and clergy delegates attend the jurisdictional conference. One of the most important things done at the jurisdictional conferences is the election of bishops.

Central Conferences

United Methodist annual conferences located outside the United States are organized into central conferences, which are similar to jurisdictional conferences.

There are seven central conferences: Africa, Central and Southern Europe, Congo, Germany, Northern Europe, Philippines, and West Africa.

The General Conference

The General Conference is the only body that has authority to speak on behalf of the entire United Methodist Church. The General Conference meets every four years to consider the business and mission of the church. It is made up of an equal number of lay and clergy delegates, who are elected from the annual conferences.

General Agencies

The general agencies of The United Methodist Church include a variety of boards, councils, committees, and commissions that are created by and responsible to the General Conference. These general agencies provide services and ministries beyond the local church and enable a common vision, mission, and ministry throughout the connectional system. The agencies include

- General Board of Church and Society
- General Board of Discipleship
- General Board of Global Ministries
- General Board of Higher Education and Ministry
- General Commission on Christian Unity and Inter-religious Concerns

- General Commission on Religion and Race
- General Commission on United Methodist Men
- General Commission on the Status and Role of Women
- General Board of Pension and Health Benefits
- The United Methodist Publishing House
- General Commission on Archives and History
- General Commission on Communication

The Book of Discipline

The Book of Discipline of The United Methodist Church contains the rules that govern the operation of the denomination. The *Discipline* also includes the history of the church and, perhaps most important, outlines the doctrines and theology of the church.

The Book of Discipline is revised every four years at the meeting of the General Conference. Petitions from individual church members, local churches, and general agencies, boards, commissions, and councils are reviewed and voted on to determine what changes will be made and what new things will be added to the official *Book of Discipline of The United Methodist Church*.

For Personal Reflection

Who is the lay leader of your congregation? Ask him or her to tell you about the lay leader's role. What district are you part of? What is the name of your annual conference? Who is your district superintendent and your bishop? Your pastor or lay leader can help you answer these questions.

Some Interesting Details

How easily may we see the hand of God in small things as well as great![1]

(*John Wesley, 1760*)

The Cross and Flame

The official insignia of The United Methodist Church is the Cross and Flame.[2] These two traditional symbols relate the church both to Christ (the cross) and to the Holy Spirit (the flame). The tongues of the flame recall the presence of the Holy Spirit at Pentecost. In addition, the dual tongues represent the merger of The Evangelical United Brethren Church and The Methodist Church in 1968 to form The United Methodist Church.

The Circuit Rider

John Wesley traveled about five thousand miles a year on horseback spreading his message of "scriptural holiness" throughout England, as well as Wales, Scotland, and Ireland. Horseback riding also became part of the life of the Methodist preachers in the American frontier. Francis Asbury organized America into large circuits. The Methodist preachers rode on horseback to establish churches, to organize new congregations, and to preach at each place along the circuits regularly. The circuit system worked well on the American frontier, and the work of the circuit riders helped establish Methodist churches in America.

Today, the pioneer circuit rider in a circle,[3] which represents the world, is a registered trademark associated with The United Methodist Publishing House.

 Cokesbury

Cokesbury

At the Christmas Conference in 1784, Thomas Coke and Francis Asbury became the first bishops of the Methodists in the United States. Together, their names are remembered in the name given to the official bookstores of The United Methodist Church: Cokesbury.

Why Methodist?

John Wesley and his brother Charles were leaders of a small group of serious Christian students at Oxford. Others made fun of this group by calling them such names as Bible Bigots, The Bible Moths, and The Enthusiasts. The group was also known as the Holy Club.

As the Holy Club continued to follow John and Charles Wesley's lead to use their time wisely and to live methodically, studying, praying, and serving others according to carefully laid plans, the name Methodists was added to the taunts of those who ridiculed them.

The name Methodist stuck, and that name has remained part of the church's name from the days of the earliest Methodist societies in England until the days of The United Methodist Church all over the world today.

Why United Methodist?

The Evangelical United Brethren Church and The Methodist Church united on April 23, 1968, to create a new denomination: The United Methodist Church. The word *United* is taken from the historical name of the EUB tradition, but it is also a descriptive name that describes the merger of these two denominations into one.

Charles Wesley: Hymn Writer

Charles Wesley wrote thousands of hymns during his ministry. Among Charles Wesley's hymns are some of the best-known and well-loved hymns that are still being sung in The United Methodist Church and in churches of many other denominations. Some of the hymns Charles Wesley wrote include

- "O for a Thousand Tongues to Sing"
- "Hark! The Herald Angels Sing"
- "Christ the Lord Is Risen Today"
- "Come, Thou Long-Expected Jesus"
- "Love Divine, All Loves Excelling"
- "I Want a Principle Within"
- "O Love Divine, What Hast Thou Done"
- "A Charge to Keep I Have"
- "Jesus, Lover of My Soul"
- "And Are We Yet Alive"

The Ministry of All Christians

All Christians are called by God, through their baptism, to be in ministry in the world. Therefore, the term *minister* is appropriately used to describe any Christian who responds to God's call to reach out to the world and its people through loving acts of service. The ministers of the church are called to serve in a variety of ways.

As Laity—From its earliest days, Methodism has been a lay movement. The term *laity* comes from *laos,* which means of the people. The laity are the whole people of God, who serve as ministers witnessing to the work of God in individual lives and in the world.

As Clergy—Within the body of all Christian ministers, though, some are called to fulfill a specific ministry through the church.

- **Deacons**—ordained ministers appointed to focus on servanthood. A deacon models the relationship between worship in the community of faith and service to God in the world. Deacons serve in a variety of ministry settings, both in the church and in the world.
- **Elders**—ordained ministers appointed to lead congregations of Christians in the celebration of the sacraments and to guide and care for the life of the community. Some elders may also serve in extension ministries beyond the local church.
- **Local Pastors**—licensed ministers appointed to perform the duties of a pastor in a specific church or charge.

Episcopal Leaders

The United Methodist Church operates under an episcopal system. Episcopal leaders, called bishops, are not a separate order of the church but are elected from among the ordained elders of the church to provide oversight and supervision for the spiritual and temporal activities of the church. Bishops are called to
- provide spiritual leadership for laity and clergy;
- interpret the faith with a prophetic voice;
- teach and uphold the traditions of the church;
- strengthen relationships with other faith communities;
- preside over the meetings of the conferences—annual, jurisdictional, central, and general;
- form the districts within an annual conference and appoint district superintendents;

- make appointments within annual conferences;
- consecrate bishops and ordain elders and deacons;
- commission probationary members of an annual conference, deaconesses, and missionaries.

College of Bishops—all the bishops of a specific jurisdiction or central conference.

Council of Bishops—all the bishops of The United Methodist Church.

Itinerant Ministry

All United Methodist clergy—local pastors, deacons, and elders—are appointed to a place for ministry by a bishop. Elders, however, are appointed as part of an appointment system known as *itinerancy,* a word derived from a word that means travel.

Methodism began with a group of traveling preachers, who went from place to place preaching, baptizing, and presiding over church affairs. That heritage has continued to today's itinerant system for the appointment of elders. Each year the bishop of an area "fixes the appointments" of the itinerant clergy (the elders) in the episcopal area as well as the appointments of the deacons and the local pastors, who are non-itinerant clergy.

Matching the gifts of an elder and the needs of the church is the most important consideration in the making of appointments. When needs change, the itinerant system provides for new appointments to be made smoothly.

Another important feature of the itinerant system is that it provides an opportunity for churches to experience a variety of leadership and ministry styles through the years, strengthening the skills of the laity whose strong leadership is essential to any ministry.

Through a commitment to open itinerancy, the connectional system of The United Methodist Church is apparent. Open itinerancy means that appointment decisions are related to gifts and needs, rather than to race, ethnic origin, gender, color, disability, marital status, or age.

The World Is My Parish

These words are a popular paraphrase of John Wesley's words.

Wesley did not set out to start a new church. In fact, when he first started preaching in the streets and fields, he questioned whether it was the right thing to do. He once wrote: "I should have thought the saving of souls almost a sin, if it had not been done in a church."[4]

But when John Wesley was no longer allowed to preach in the church, he decided that "seeing I have now no parish of my own, nor probably ever shall...I look upon all the world as my parish...This is the work which I know God has called me to."[5]

Today, United Methodists join John Wesley in declaring that the whole world is our parish.

Endnotes

1 From "Journal From May 6, 1760, to October 28, 1762," journal entry on August 7, 1760, by John Wesley.

2 The Cross and Flame is a registered trademark, and the use is supervised by the General Council on Finance and Administration of The United Methodist Church. Permission to use the Cross and Flame must be obtained from the General Council on Finance and Administration of The United Methodist Church—Legal Department, 1200 Davis Street, Evanston, IL 60201.

3 The Circuit Rider is a registered trademark of The United Methodist Publishing House. Used by permission.

4 From "Journal From August 12, 1738, to November 1, 1739," journal entry on March 31, 1739, by John Wesley.

5 From "Journal From August 12, 1738, to November 1, 1739," journal entry on June 11, 1739, by John Wesley.

Going Further

And are we yet alive, and see each other's face? Glory and thanks to Jesus give for his almighty grace![1]

(*Charles Wesley, 1749*)

These words from Charles Wesley's hymn are the traditional opening words of annual conference meetings throughout The United Methodist Church. If you are just beginning your journey into the history of the denomination, it is probably hard to imagine that the stories and facts and feelings you have experienced in these few pages are only a beginning. But there are many more stories to tell and many more ideas to explore—from the days of John Wesley all the way to today in your local church.

Learn More

- Read more about John Wesley and those who followed him.
- Study the doctrines and theology of The United Methodist Church.

- Learn the history of your own local congregation.
- Learn how to use *The Book of Discipline, The Book of Resolutions, The United Methodist Hymnal* (or other official hymnals), and the United Methodist website.

Get Involved

- What is your congregation doing to fulfill the mission of The United Methodist Church—to make disciples of Jesus Christ?
- In what district and annual conference is your church?
- Who is your district superintendent? your bishop?
- Who represents your local congregation in the meetings of your annual conference?
- Who represents your conference at the General Conference?
- When and where will the next General Conference be held?

Keep It Alive

- Get involved in the ministry of your congregation by welcoming new people to the church, by nurturing them, and by sending them out to make disciples.
- Teach the students in your class about their rich heritage as United Methodists.

Endnote

1 From "And Are We Yet Alive," by Charles Wesley (1749).

Helpful Resources

Websites

General Board of Discipleship of The United Methodist Church (www.gbod.org). On this site you will find articles related to discipleship and teaching. Particular sites of interest are www.gbod.org/education and www.gbod.org/keepingintouch.

Discipleship Resources (www.discipleshipresources.org). In this online bookstore you can purchase additional copies of this booklet, other booklets in the series, and other books published by Discipleship Resources.

The United Methodist Church (www.umc.org). On this site you can find news articles related to the United Methodist denomination, as well as official church responses to current events. You can also locate your annual conference's web page and find out what's happening in your area.

Official Resources
The United Methodist Publishing House

The Book of Discipline of The United Methodist Church—2000

The Book of Resolutions of The United Methodist Church—2000

The United Methodist Book of Worship

Guidelines for Leading Your Church

The United Methodist Directory and Index of Resources

Hymnals
- — *The United Methodist Hymnal*
- — *Mil Voces Para Celebrar: Himnario Metodista*
- — *Come, Let Us Worship: The Korean-English United Methodist Hymnal*

Books
Discipleship Resources

A Brief History of The United Methodist Church (1998).

A Brief Introduction to the Book of Discipline of The United Methodist Church, by Branson L. Thurston (1998).

Living Deeply Our New Life in Christ: A Wesleyan Spirituality for Today, by Jerry L. Mercer (2000).

Living Our Beliefs: The United Methodist Way, by Kenneth L. Carder (1997).

The United Methodist Member's Handbook (Revised and Expanded), by George E. Koehler (1997).

The United Methodist Primer (2001 Revised Edition), by Chester E. Custer (2001).

The United Methodist Way, by Branson L. Thurston (1983).

Abingdon Press

Grace Sufficient: A History of Women in American Methodism, 1760–1968, by Jean Miller Schmidt (1999).

John Wesley: Holiness of Heart & Life, by Charles Yrigoyen, Jr. (1999).

United Methodist Communications

Sharing God's Gifts: A United Methodist Handbook, 2001–2004 (2001).

Ordering Resources

Resources published by Discipleship Resources may be ordered online at www.discipleshipresources.org; by phone at 800-685-4370; by fax at 770-442-9742; or by mail from Discipleship Resources Distribution Center, P.O. Box 1616, Alpharetta, GA 30009-1616.

Resources published by Abingdon Press and official United Methodist Resources can be ordered by calling Cokesbury.

Resources published by United Methodist Communications can by ordered by calling 888-862-3242.